ChatGPT My Co-Pilot

Master AI to Crush Work & Organize Life

© **2025** ChatGPT Is My Co-Pilot: All rights reserved. No part of this publication may be reproduced, stored in a retrieval system, or transmitted in any form or by any means—electronic, mechanical, photocopying, recording, or otherwise —without the prior written permission of the author.

Contents

Part I: Getting Started with ChatGPT

- Chapter 1: Let's Get You Set Up (No Tech Degree Required) Page — 10

Part II: ChatGPT at Work

- Chapter 2: ChatGPT at Work – Your New Productivity Wingman Page — 16

- Chapter 3: Plan It, Manage It, Crush It (With ChatGPT on Your Side) Page — 27

- Chapter 4: ChatGPT for Marketing, Sales & Customer Stuff   Page — 37

- Chapter 5: Solopreneurs & Side Hustlers – You Don't Have to Do It All Alone Page — 48

Part III: ChatGPT for Everyday Life

- Chapter 6: Home Life, Handled – Your Everyday AI Assistant   Page — 58
- Chapter 7: Parenting with AI – Because You Deserve Backup   Page — 69

Part IV: Personal Growth, Creativity & Relationships

- Chapter 8: ChatGPT – Your Personal Growth & Hobby Buddy   Page — 81
- Chapter 9: Real Connections, Real Conversations – Using ChatGPT to Support Your Relationships & Social Life   Page — 88

Part V: Leveling Up Your AI Game

- Chapter 10: Getting the Most from ChatGPT – Prompt Like a Pro, Customize Like a Boss   Page — 97

Wrap-Up & Extras

- Final Thoughts: You've Got the Tool—Now Make It Yours   Page — 106
- Power Prompts Toolkit   Page — 108

Introduction:

Let's Be Real—You're Probably Not Using ChatGPT to Its Full Potential

Let me guess: you've heard about ChatGPT. Maybe even tried it once or twice. Asked it something random, got a weirdly smart (or slightly off) answer, and then moved on.

Or maybe you've seen coworkers, friends, or your favorite YouTubers swear by it—talking about how it's changed how they work, how they write, how they plan their day. And now you're wondering, *"Okay... what am I missing?"*

You're in the right place.

This book is for you—the curious, busy human who doesn't have time to figure out all the techy stuff, but knows deep down that there's something powerful here. Because there is. ChatGPT isn't just a fancy chatbot. It's a personal assistant, writing coach, brainstorm buddy, meal planner, idea generator, and maybe even your new secret weapon—if you know how to use it right.

Why I Wrote This

When ChatGPT first came out, I was fascinated. And a little skeptical. I started messing around with it—writing emails, outlining projects, planning my week, even asking it what to cook for dinner with whatever random stuff was in my fridge.

Pretty quickly, I realized: **this thing can save serious time.**

But here's the deal—most people don't get past the first few "Hey, what can you do?" kind of questions. And that's a shame, because they're leaving SO much value on the table.

So I decided to write the guide I wish someone had handed me when I first started using ChatGPT: no tech jargon, no complicated theory. Just real-life ways you can use this tool at **work** and at **home** to make life easier, smoother, and maybe even a little more fun.

Who This Book Is For

This book is for regular people—no coding background required. If you:

- Juggle a full-time job and a full inbox,
- Run a household and always feel one step behind,
- Have a side hustle, a creative spark, or a million tabs open in your brain,
- Or just want to spend less time doing repetitive stuff...

Then yeah, this book's for you.

What You'll Get

- A friendly intro to ChatGPT (no, you don't need to be a techie)
- Real examples of how to use it in everyday life
- Time-saving tricks for your job, your home, and everything in between
- A simple way to think about AI—not as something scary or overwhelming, but as a tool you *already* have access to

We're going to keep it casual, practical, and (hopefully) a little fun. This isn't about learning a whole new language. It's about making your life easier, one prompt at a time.

Sound good?

Let's dive in. You're going to be amazed at what this thing can do.

Chapter 1:

Let's Get You Set Up

(No Tech Degree Required)

Alright—so you're ready to bring ChatGPT into your life. Great move.

Now, if you're thinking, *"But I'm not a tech person!"*—don't stress. This chapter is your no-jargon, no-pressure walkthrough of what ChatGPT actually is, how to access it, and how to start using it for real-world tasks (like, today).

What Even *Is* ChatGPT?

Let's keep it simple. ChatGPT is like a supercharged chatbot that you can talk to like a friend, co-worker, or personal assistant. You type something in, it responds. The magic? It's trained on a mountain of information and can help you write, brainstorm, organize, explain things, and a whole lot more.

It's not perfect—it'll sometimes get things wrong (we'll talk about that)—but when you learn how to ask it the right way, it can become your secret weapon.

Step 1: Signing Up

You don't need to install anything weird. Just head over to **chat.openai.com** and make a free account.

✨ **TIP:** Want the best experience? Use a laptop for the first time—bigger screen, easier typing. Once you're comfy, grab the ChatGPT app on your phone to use it on the go.

There's a **free version (GPT-3.5)** and a **paid version (GPT-4)**—about $20/month at the time of writing. The free version is *totally fine* for most things, especially when you're just getting started.

GPT-4 is smarter, better at reasoning, and remembers what you told it (kind of like a super intern who actually listens). If you find yourself using ChatGPT a lot, the upgrade might be worth it later.

Step 2: Meet Your New Sidekick

The chat window is just a blank box at first. Don't be intimidated—this is where the fun starts.

You can type things like:

- "Help me write a professional-sounding email to my boss asking for a day off."
- "What are some healthy dinner ideas for picky kids?"

- "Can you help me plan a 3-day trip to New York on a budget?"

And ChatGPT will respond like a helpful assistant. You can ask it to change things, rewrite them, or give you more ideas. It's like talking to someone who *always* has something useful to say.

Step 3: Understanding Prompts (aka, What You Type In)

You'll hear the word "prompt" a lot. That's just the fancy term for whatever you type into the chat box.

Good prompts are:

- Clear
- Specific
- Conversational

For example:

❌ "Help me." → Too vague
✅ "I need help writing a quick summary of today's Zoom meeting for my team."

Want to really level up? Try telling ChatGPT *who it should be*:

- "Act like a productivity coach and help me organize my week."
- "Pretend you're a parent of two and give me ideas for indoor weekend activities."

Boom. That's prompt magic.

Real Talk: What Can You Actually Use This For?

Here are a few ways to test-drive it right now:

- Draft an email (work or personal)
- Get dinner ideas based on what's in your fridge
- Summarize a long article or email
- Ask it to explain something like you're five
- Get a pep talk when you're feeling blah (seriously—it's weirdly good at this)

But Wait... Is It Private?

Great question. ChatGPT doesn't *store* or *share* your chats publicly, but **don't feed it sensitive stuff** like bank info, passwords, or anything you wouldn't want a random stranger seeing. Play it safe.

If you're using GPT-4, you can turn off the memory function in your settings if you want it to "forget" your conversations.

Quick Recap:

☑ Sign up at chat.openai.com
☑ Start with free GPT-3.5 (upgrade later if you want)
☑ Just type like you're chatting with a friend
☑ Be specific, give it a role if you like
☑ Have fun and explore

In the next chapter, we'll dive into all the **work-related stuff** ChatGPT can help with—like emails, reports, meeting prep, and those annoying "Can you just write something quick?" tasks.

But for now, go play around. Ask it something fun. Try it out. You literally can't break it.

Chapter 2:

ChatGPT at Work – Your New Productivity Wingman

Let's be honest—work can get overwhelming. Emails pile up, meetings run long, and somehow your to-do list is longer at the end of the day than it was in the morning. Sound familiar?

What if I told you that you could cut your mental workload in half just by having a smart assistant help you out… and you don't even have to hire anyone?

This is where ChatGPT comes in.

Whether you're working a 9-to-5, running a business, or freelancing from your favorite coffee shop, this little AI can help you *get more done in less time*—without losing your mind in the process.

1. Emails—Finally Not a Chore

If writing emails is your personal version of a nightmare, you're not alone. The good news? ChatGPT is *really* good at this.

Try prompts like:

- "Write a polite email to a client asking for an update on their project."
- "Make this email sound more confident but still friendly."
- "Turn this list of bullet points into a short update email for my team."

You can even copy-paste a rough draft and ask it to clean it up:

"Here's what I wrote. Make it sound more professional and fix the grammar."

It's like having a built-in editor who doesn't judge you for typos.

2. Reports, Summaries & Meeting Notes

You know those tasks where you have to take a bunch of messy info and turn it into something clean and presentable? Yeah—ChatGPT loves that.

Examples:

- "Summarize these meeting notes into 3 bullet points per topic."

- "Turn this spreadsheet data into a one-paragraph progress update."
- "Write a short report based on this info for my manager."

And if you're in a meeting-heavy job, this is a game changer:

Copy your raw notes, paste them in, and ask: "Can you organize this into a clean summary with action items?"

Boom. Instant clarity.

3. Brainstorming Partner (That Doesn't Shoot Down Your Ideas)

Feeling stuck? Need ideas? ChatGPT is surprisingly creative.

You can ask it things like:

- "Give me 10 content ideas for my business blog."
- "What are some creative ways to announce a product launch?"
- "I need icebreaker ideas for a virtual team meeting."

You can even bounce ideas off it like a real coworker:

"I'm thinking about launching an online course. Can you help me come up with a name, a structure, and marketing ideas?"

And the best part? It never says, "That won't work."

4. Organizing Your Day or Week

ChatGPT can help you figure out how to manage your time better:

- "Here's everything I need to get done this week—can you organize it into a schedule?"
- "Help me time-block my day around 2 meetings at 10am and 3pm."
- "Suggest a morning routine to help me focus."

It won't drag you out of bed (sadly), but it can give you a plan.

5. Templates, Scripts & Docs (Without Starting From Scratch)

Starting with a blank page is the worst. So... don't.

Let ChatGPT give you a starting point:

- "Create a project proposal template for a freelance graphic designer."
- "Write a job description for a remote customer support role."
- "Draft a client onboarding checklist for a small agency."

Even if you don't use the whole thing, you'll save loads of time just by not starting from zero.

🛠️ Real Talk: Will It Replace Jobs?

This comes up a lot, so let's be honest: ChatGPT isn't here to *replace* you—it's here to *support* you. The people who get ahead will be the ones who **learn how to work with AI**, not run from it.

It's like using a calculator for math. You still need to understand what's going on—but now you've got a tool to speed it up.

So use ChatGPT to work smarter, not harder. Take the time you save and spend it doing more meaningful work, or hey—just go outside for once. 😌

🚀 Try This Before the Next Chapter:

Here's a mini challenge:

1. Pick a real work task you have to do this week

2. Open ChatGPT

3. Ask it to help you write, plan, or organize it

Just see what it gives you. You might be surprised how good it is.

To wrap this chapter up here are some ChatGPT work prompts you can use

ChatGPT Work Prompts

Cheat Sheet

Quick Prompts to Save Time & Boost Productivity at Work

Email Prompts

- "Write a professional email requesting a deadline extension on a project."

- "Reply politely to an unhappy client and offer a solution."

- "Turn these bullet points into a team update email: [paste bullet points]."

- "Make this email sound more confident: [paste your draft]."

Reports, Docs & Meeting Notes

- "Summarize these meeting notes into action items and key points: [paste notes]."

- "Create a weekly project status update for a team of 5."

- "Turn this rough draft into a polished project proposal."
- "Organize this list of tasks into a progress report for my manager."

Brainstorming & Ideas

- "Give me 10 blog post ideas for a real estate business."
- "Suggest creative ways to announce a product launch."
- "Help me brainstorm a name for a digital marketing agency."
- "Act like a brand strategist—what's a cool tagline for this product: [describe product]?"

Planning & Time Management

- "Organize these tasks into a daily schedule: [list your tasks]."
- "Help me time-block my workday around 2 meetings at 11am and 3pm."

- "Create a focused morning routine for someone who works remotely."

- "Break down this big project into weekly milestones."

Templates & Checklists

- "Create a new client onboarding checklist for a web design business."

- "Write a social media content calendar template for a small business."

- "Draft a contract outline for freelance writing services."

- "Give me a cold outreach script for potential clients."

🧠 Bonus Power Tips

- Start prompts with:
    - "Act like a..." (e.g. productivity coach, marketing expert, HR manager)
    - "Help me..." (e.g. brainstorm, write, organize, fix, rewrite)
- Follow up with:

- "Make it shorter."

- "Add a friendly tone."

- "Give me 3 options."

- "Now make it funnier/more formal/more concise."

✅ **Pro Tip**: Save your favorite prompts in a doc or notes app. Build your own "ChatGPT Playbook" over time!

Coming up next, we're going to look at how ChatGPT can help **small business owners, freelancers, and side hustlers**. If you've got a business (or are thinking about starting one), it's about to become your favorite brainstorming partner, content writer, and virtual assistant—all rolled into one.

Let's keep going.

Chapter 3:

Plan It, Manage It, Crush It (With ChatGPT on Your Side)

We all know that *planning* is important... but let's be real—it can feel like a full-time job just keeping track of your actual job.

There's the project timeline, team tasks, deadlines, last-minute changes, and that one person who always "didn't see the email." 😅

The good news? ChatGPT is surprisingly great at helping you plan and manage projects—big or small. Whether you're working solo, leading a team, or just trying to organize your own brain, this chapter will show you how to make ChatGPT your project co-pilot.

📋 1. Build a To-Do List That Actually Makes Sense

Ever sit down to work and spend half the time figuring out what you're supposed to do first?

You can feed ChatGPT a rough list and let it turn it into something useful.

Try:

"Here's everything I need to get done this week. Can you break it down by day and prioritize it?"

Or:

"Help me turn this messy list into a clear, actionable to-do list: [paste tasks]"

You can even ask it to organize by urgency, category, or energy level (yes, really):

- "Sort these tasks by which ones I can do quickly vs. which need deep focus."

📅 2. Plan a Full Project Timeline

Need to plan out a launch, campaign, event, or multi-week project? ChatGPT can help build out a timeline step-by-step.

Try something like:

"Help me create a 4-week project plan to launch a new online course. Include weekly goals and daily task ideas."

Or:

"Build a simple Gantt-style breakdown for a product launch in May with these phases: [list phases]."

Boom. Instant project skeleton.

Then you can tweak it, add deadlines, and share it with your team (or just use it to stay sane yourself).

🔄 3. Delegate Like a Boss (Even If You're a Team of One)

If you're managing people or working with collaborators, ChatGPT can help you:

- Assign tasks
- Write instructions
- Clarify who's doing what

Example:

"Create a task breakdown for a team of 3 working on a website redesign. One is a designer, one is a copywriter, one is a developer."

Or:

"Write an email assigning roles and deadlines for this marketing campaign: [describe project]."

It's like having a project manager whispering helpful suggestions in your ear—without the micromanaging.

✎ 4. Notes, Docs & Recaps Made Easy

You had a meeting. You scribbled down 17 half-thoughts and 2 doodles. Now what?

ChatGPT to the rescue:

- "Turn these notes into a meeting summary with action steps."

- "Write a client update based on these project details: [paste notes or bullet points]."

- "Summarize this conversation into a weekly progress report."

And yes—it can even help make boring updates sound... not boring.

⚙ 5. Automating the Small Stuff

Want to go even further? If you're using tools like **Notion**, **Trello**, **Google Docs**, or **Slack**, ChatGPT can help write updates, content, or even build templates for you.

Examples:

- "Write a Slack update to let the team know Task X is done and ready for review."

- "Help me structure a Notion page for tracking client projects."

And if you get into tools like **Zapier**, **Make.com**, or **ChatGPT plugins**, you can start automating parts of your workflow. But don't worry—we'll keep it simple for now.

🧠 Real Talk: The Planning Trap

Here's a gentle warning: planning is great, but don't get *stuck* in planning. ChatGPT can give you beautiful checklists, roadmaps, and timelines—but execution is still on you. 💪

Use it to organize, simplify, and clarify. Then go take action.

(And hey, you can even ask ChatGPT for motivation if you're dragging: "Give me a short pep talk for getting started on a big project.")

✅ Try This Before the Next Chapter:

1. Pick a real project you're working on (work, side hustle, anything).
2. Ask ChatGPT to break it down into phases, tasks, or a schedule.

3. Tweak it, personalize it—and try using it as your new plan for the week.

📝 Planning Prompts Cheat Sheet

Use ChatGPT to plan, prioritize, and power through projects

✅ Task & To-Do List Prompts

- "Here's my to-do list for the week. Can you break it down by day and prioritize the tasks?"

- "Sort this list of tasks into categories: urgent, important, optional."

- "Turn this list into a checklist I can use in Notion: [paste tasks]."

- "Organize my daily tasks into a time-blocked schedule."

📅 Project Timeline Prompts

- "Help me create a 4-week plan to launch a new product."

- "Break down this project into weekly phases: [describe project]."

- "Build a simple project timeline with these milestones: [list milestones]."

- "Suggest a schedule for writing, editing, and launching a blog series."

👥 Team Planning & Delegation Prompts

- "Split this project into 3 roles: designer, writer, and developer. Assign tasks to each."

- "Write a short message assigning roles and deadlines to a team."

- "Create a shared task tracker format I can use with my team."

- "Write a project kickoff checklist for a remote team."

📝 Docs, Notes & Recap Prompts

- "Turn these messy meeting notes into a clean summary: [paste notes]."

- "Summarize this week's project updates into 3 bullet points per topic."

- "Draft a status update email based on this list of progress points."

- "Write a weekly recap for my boss that sounds clear and proactive."

Routine & Process Prompts

- "Help me design a simple weekly workflow to manage client projects."

- "Suggest a Monday morning routine to plan my week."

- "Create a recurring project checklist I can use every month."

- "Write a process document for onboarding new freelance clients."

Bonus Role-Based Prompts

Use these to get next-level structure:

- "Act like a project manager. Help me organize this campaign step-by-step."

- "Pretend you're a time management coach. Plan my week for maximum focus."

- "You're a productivity expert—how can I plan this event without burning out?"

- "Act like a startup founder. What should I focus on first when launching a new service?"

Pro Tip: Once ChatGPT gives you a plan, ask:

- "Add checkboxes so I can track it."
- "Turn this into a timeline."
- "Simplify this into just 5 key action steps."
- "Turn this into a shareable doc format."

Next up? We're diving into how ChatGPT can **supercharge your content, marketing, and customer communication**—from social media posts to product descriptions and beyond. If you run a business, do freelance work, or just want to sound better online, you'll love this next chapter.

Chapter 4:

ChatGPT for Marketing, Sales & Customer Stuff

(Without the Headache)

Let's be real—marketing can be a lot. Between coming up with content, writing emails, staying "on brand," and trying to sound like a human being while also *selling something*, it's easy to get stuck or overwhelmed.

Whether you're running a business, freelancing, or just promoting a side hustle, ChatGPT can help you create better content, connect with your audience, and save hours each week.

Seriously, it's like hiring a creative team... for free.

📣 1. Write Social Media Content Without Staring at a Blank Screen

You don't have to be a social media expert—or even like social media—to let ChatGPT help you show up online.

Try prompts like:

- "Write 5 Instagram captions for a productivity coach promoting her new course."

- "Give me 10 tweet ideas to promote a free eBook on healthy habits."

- "Create a week of social media posts for a dog grooming business."

You can even ask it to adjust the tone:

- "Make it sound funny and casual."

- "Rewrite this post in a more inspiring tone."

- "Add emojis and a call to action."

♥ 2. Emails That Actually Get Opened (and Clicked)

You can use ChatGPT for all kinds of email help—newsletters, cold pitches, follow-ups, launch announcements, and more.

Examples:

- "Write a welcome email for new subscribers to my email list."

- "Create a 3-part email sequence to launch my online course."

- "Write a follow-up email after a discovery call with a client."

And of course:

"Make it shorter."
"Add urgency."
"Change the subject line to improve open rates."

It's your personal email marketing assistant—without the agency fees.

3. Product Descriptions That Sell (Without Sounding Like a Robot)

Selling something? Let ChatGPT help describe it in a way that's clear, engaging, and persuasive.

Prompt ideas:

- "Write a short product description for a handmade soy candle with a calming lavender scent."
- "Create a playful description for a planner designed for busy moms."
- "Explain this service like you're talking to a friend: [insert details]."

You can even ask for multiple versions:

- "Give me 3 styles: formal, casual, and funny."

4. Answer Customer Questions Like a Pro

No one loves writing customer service replies, but ChatGPT makes it painless.

Try:

- "Write a polite response to a customer asking for a refund after the return window has passed."
- "Create a helpful reply to someone asking how to use our product."
- "Turn these FAQs into a friendly response template."

Want to go the extra mile? Ask:

"Make it sound friendly and empathetic."
"Include a link to our help page."
"Add a suggestion for a similar product."

5. Build a Quick Content Plan (That You'll Actually Use)

Instead of winging your marketing week by week, let ChatGPT help you map things out.

Try:

- "Create a 30-day content calendar for a small fitness brand."

- "Build a blog post plan for a personal finance coach targeting millennials."

- "Help me come up with a monthly marketing plan for my Etsy shop."

You can break it down by channel (Instagram, blog, email), by theme (inspiration, how-to, promo), or even by goal (engagement vs. sales).

🔥 Real Talk: Authenticity Still Matters

Here's the deal—ChatGPT is powerful, but people can spot a "copy-paste AI" post from a mile away. So use it to get started, spark ideas, or polish your message—but don't forget to add **your voice**.

You're not trying to sound like a robot. You're trying to sound like *you*—just with a little help from a very fast-thinking friend.

☑ **Try This Before the Next Chapter:**

1. Pick one thing you're promoting—product, service, event, anything.

2. Ask ChatGPT to help write 3 pieces of content about it:

    o One social media post

    o One short email

    o One product or service description

3. Edit it, personalize it, and send it out. Boom—done.

📎 Marketing Prompts Cheat Sheet

Write faster, sell smarter, and connect better—with a little help from AI

📣 Social Media Prompts

- "Write 5 Instagram captions for [type of business] with a friendly, casual tone."

- "Create a week of LinkedIn posts for a freelancer offering [your service]."

- "Give me 10 short, engaging tweets about [topic or product]."

- "Turn this blog post into 3 social media snippets: [paste text]."

- "Add emojis and a call to action to this Instagram caption: [paste caption]."

💙 Email Prompts

- "Write a welcome email for new subscribers who just downloaded my free checklist."

- "Create a 3-part email sequence to promote my [course/product/service]."

- "Write a short follow-up email after a discovery call with a potential client."

- "Make this newsletter more personal and conversational: [paste text]."

- "Suggest 5 subject lines for this promo email: [paste email copy]."

🛍️ Product & Service Descriptions

- "Write a product description for [insert item] in a fun, modern tone."

- "Explain this offer like you're talking to a friend: [describe it in plain words]."

- "Give me 3 versions of this description: casual, elegant, and bold."

- "Rewrite this to highlight benefits, not features: [paste description]."

- "Add urgency and a limited-time offer line at the end."

💬 Customer Service & FAQ Prompts

- "Write a friendly response to a refund request outside the return window."

- "Turn these FAQs into short, helpful answers: [paste questions]."

- "Draft a reply to a customer asking if your product is eco-friendly."

- "Make this response more empathetic and warm: [paste response]."

- "Create a canned response template for common product questions."

🧠 Content Strategy Prompts

- "Create a 30-day content calendar for a solopreneur who offers [your service]."

- "Build a blog post plan with 1 post per week for the next 2 months."

- "Suggest 5 lead magnet ideas for [your niche or industry]."

- "Act like a content strategist. What should I post to attract [target audience]?"

- "Help me build a monthly marketing plan for [business or brand]."

✨ Prompt Tweaks to Try

- "Make it shorter."
- "Add a hook at the beginning."
- "Include a call to action."
- "Make it sound more like [brand voice or person]."
- "Add humor / make it more inspirational / sound more premium."

✅ **Pro Tip**: Save your best-performing prompts and results in a doc—your personal AI-powered swipe file is now officially a thing.

Chapter 5:

Solopreneurs & Side Hustlers — You Don't Have to Do It All Alone

Running your own thing is exciting, but let's be honest—it's also exhausting.

You're the marketer, the customer support team, the product creator, the social media manager, the accountant... oh, and sometimes the actual human who needs sleep. 😅

But here's the good news: you're no longer *completely* on your own.

ChatGPT can be your silent business partner—the one that never complains, doesn't need coffee breaks, and is always down to brainstorm at 2 AM.

🧠 1. Turn Your Ideas Into Offers (Faster)

Have an idea for a course, service, or product but don't know where to start? ChatGPT can help flesh it out.

Try:

- "Help me outline a digital course for beginner photographers."
- "Act like a business coach. Help me turn my coaching idea into a paid offer."
- "Break this business idea into steps: [describe your idea]."

You can go from idea → structure → marketing plan in a single session.

✎ 2. Write Sales Pages, Bios & About Sections

Hate writing about yourself? Same. But ChatGPT's got your back.

Prompts to try:

- "Write a friendly, professional bio for a freelance graphic designer."
- "Create a sales page for a 4-week productivity bootcamp."
- "Help me describe my service like I'm talking to a potential client."

It'll give you a first draft you can personalize and polish without getting stuck in the "what do I even say?" spiral.

🛒 3. Sell Without Feeling Sleazy

Marketing doesn't have to feel gross or pushy. Ask ChatGPT to help you sound natural and confident.

Examples:

- "Write a soft-sell email promoting my coaching program."
- "Create a value-based pitch for my Etsy shop that focuses on benefits."
- "Give me 3 different ways to promote my product without sounding salesy."

Then tweak the language until it feels *like you*—just a little more polished.

📈 4. Plan Your Content & Campaigns

You can ask ChatGPT to help you build content *and* organize it in a way that fits your vibe and schedule.

Try:

- "Create a 4-week content plan for a productivity coach promoting her new ebook."

- "Suggest weekly themes for my blog as a career mentor."

- "Help me plan a simple launch campaign for my online workshop."

You'll have more strategy in less time—and with way fewer headaches.

🤖 5. Automate the Boring Stuff (or at Least Write It Faster)

Let ChatGPT handle the repetitive admin stuff so you can focus on the fun/important work.

Prompts:

- "Write a client onboarding email that explains my process and next steps."

- "Create a welcome message for new members of my private community."

- "Write a thank-you message to send after someone books a call."

Bonus: You can use those messages over and over. Copy, paste, tweak. Done.

🔄 Real Talk: You're Still the Magic

Here's the thing—AI can help you work smarter. It can write the emails, build the schedule, and help brainstorm the next big thing. But it can't *be* you.

Your voice, your energy, your story—that's what people connect with.

So use ChatGPT as your assistant, not your replacement. Let it take care of the heavy lifting so you can focus on building something that feels good, does good, and grows without burning you out.

✅ Try This Before the Next Chapter:

1. Pick one part of your business you've been avoiding (writing a bio, building a content plan, writing a pitch—whatever).

2. Ask ChatGPT to help. Use a prompt from this chapter.

3. Edit the result, make it yours, and send it out. Done is better than perfect.

Solopreneur & Side Hustler Prompts Cheat Sheet

Your AI-powered assistant for launching, marketing, and managing your biz

Turn Ideas Into Offers

- "Help me outline a 4-week coaching program for busy professionals."

- "Act like a business coach. Turn this idea into a digital product: [describe idea]."

- "What kind of service or offer could I build based on this skill set: [list skills]?"

- "Suggest 3 ways I could monetize this side hustle: [describe side hustle]."

Write Sales Pages & Bios

- "Write a compelling About Me section for a freelance copywriter with 3 years of experience."

- "Create a landing page headline for an online course about building better habits."

- "Write a product description that highlights transformation and benefits: [describe product]."

- "Give me 3 tagline options for my Etsy store selling handmade skincare."

🛍️ Sell Without Feeling Sleazy

- "Write a soft pitch for my new workshop in a friendly, helpful tone."

- "Suggest 3 non-pushy ways to promote my ebook on Instagram."

- "Turn this feature list into a benefits-focused sales message: [paste features]."

- "Rewrite this with more empathy and confidence: [paste text]."

📅 Plan Your Content & Campaigns

- "Create a 30-day Instagram content plan for a solo wellness coach."

- "Build a simple launch strategy for my online course starting next month."

- "Suggest weekly email topics for a productivity newsletter."
- "Help me map out a content plan that promotes my services without being repetitive."

📬 Write Admin & Client Messages

- "Write a client welcome email with next steps and FAQs."
- "Create a follow-up message to send after a discovery call."
- "Draft a thank-you message for customers who purchase from my shop."
- "Write a polite reminder for an unpaid invoice due last week."

🧠 Bonus Role-Based Prompts

- "Act like a creative strategist. What would you suggest I focus on this month?"
- "You're a productivity coach—how can I better manage my client workload?"

- "Pretend you're my content manager. Help me repurpose this blog post into 3 social captions."

- "Act like a launch copywriter and help me build hype for my new product."

Quick Prompt Tweaks:

- "Make it more casual/formal/inspirational."

- "Add a call to action."

- "Make it sound like me: [describe your tone]."

- "Summarize this in 2 lines for a social post."

- "Turn this into a short script for a Reel/TikTok."

✅ **Pro Tip**: Save your favorite outputs and prompts in a "Biz Content Vault" (Notion, Google Docs, etc.). You'll build your own AI-powered marketing toolkit over time!

Next up, we're flipping to the **personal side of life**—because ChatGPT isn't just a work tool. In **Chapter 6**, you'll see how it can help manage your home life, schedule, shopping list, and even your kids' homework. (Yes, really.)

Chapter 6:

Home Life, Handled — Your Everyday AI Assistant

Let's be honest—keeping a house (or apartment, or even just your brain) organized is a full-time job on its own.

Between grocery runs, meal planning, juggling appointments, cleaning schedules, random "adulting" tasks, and trying to remember where you left your keys (again), life at home can feel like chaos on repeat.

But guess what? ChatGPT isn't just for work. It can help you **run your home life like a boss**, too. In this chapter, we're talking **family logistics, personal routines, budgeting, meals, schedules**, and all the little things that keep your life moving.

🛒 1. Meal Planning (That You'll Actually Stick To)

Staring into your fridge wondering what to make—again—is exhausting. Let ChatGPT take over.

Prompts to try:

- "Plan 5 healthy dinners for a family of 4 with a picky eater."

- "Give me a grocery list based on these meals: [list meals]."

- "Create a vegetarian meal plan for two adults, with no mushrooms."

- "I have chicken, rice, and spinach—what can I cook tonight?"

Bonus: Ask it to give you recipes, prep times, and even leftovers plans.

2. Organize Your Week Like a Life Manager

ChatGPT can help you plan your week around work, school pickups, self-care, appointments, workouts—whatever your life looks like.

Try:

- "Help me schedule my week around work hours (9–5), two gym sessions, and my kids' soccer practices."

- "Create a Sunday routine to help me prep for the week."

- "Suggest a daily checklist for a productive, balanced weekday."

- "Build a weekly schedule that includes meal prep, cleaning, and downtime."

It's like having a personal planner who knows you want to actually *enjoy* your week, not just survive it.

💰 3. Budgeting & Financial Planning Help

While ChatGPT won't connect to your bank account, it can help you **plan**, **organize**, and even **talk about money** better.

Try:

- "Create a simple monthly budget for a household with $4,000 income and basic expenses."

- "Help me make a debt repayment plan with $500/month."

- "Suggest a savings strategy for someone with irregular freelance income."

- "Explain credit scores like I'm 12."

Bonus: Ask for a financial checklist, comparison shopping tips, or a script to talk about finances with a partner. (It's surprisingly helpful.)

4. Chores, Routines & Family Logistics

Whether you're flying solo or managing a whole household, routines and shared responsibilities are everything.

Prompts to try:

- "Create a weekly cleaning schedule for a 3-bedroom home."
- "Suggest a chore chart for two adults and two kids (ages 6 and 10)."
- "Build a Sunday reset checklist for a calm start to the week."
- "Make a list of age-appropriate chores for a 7-year-old."

You can even make it fun:

"Turn this into a game for my kids to help clean the house."

🎓 5. Help With Kids' Homework & Learning

Yes, ChatGPT can help with math, science, reading comprehension, writing prompts, and more—but it can also help you **help your kids** without pulling your hair out.

Try:

- "Explain fractions to a 4th grader using pizza."
- "Create a bedtime story starring a dragon and a robot who become friends."
- "Help my 12-year-old write a paragraph about the water cycle."
- "Make a fun quiz to help my kid study for a U.S. history test."

It's like having a tutor, storyteller, and quiz-maker on demand.

🧠 Real Talk: It's Not About Doing More—It's About Doing Less *Better*

You don't need more pressure. You don't need another app telling you to hustle harder. What you need is a system that helps you feel a little more in control. A little more supported.

That's what ChatGPT can be—a simple, always-there helper that makes the mental load feel lighter.

✅ Try This Before the Next Chapter:

1. Ask ChatGPT to plan your meals for the next 3 days.

2. Then ask it to build you a short, realistic weekly routine based on your real schedule.

3. Try it. Adjust it. See how it feels. (Spoiler: kinda awesome.)

Home Life Prompts Cheat Sheet

Let ChatGPT help you run your life, not just your inbox.

🍽 Meal Planning & Grocery Help

- "Plan 5 easy dinners for a family of 4 with a picky eater."

- "Create a weekly meal plan with no gluten or dairy."

- "I have ground beef, rice, and broccoli—what can I make?"

- "Give me a grocery list for these meals: [list them]."

- "Suggest lunchbox ideas for a 10-year-old that aren't sandwiches."

📝 Scheduling & Life Organization

- "Build me a weekly routine that includes work (9–5), 2 workouts, and 1 free evening."

- "Help me organize my weekend so I can clean, meal prep, and rest."

- "Create a morning routine for a busy parent with kids."

- "Suggest a daily checklist that helps me stay productive but not overwhelmed."

🧹 Cleaning, Chores & Home Upkeep

- "Write a weekly cleaning schedule for a 3-bedroom house."
- "Suggest a family chore chart for two parents and two kids (ages 6 and 9)."
- "Create a Sunday reset checklist to start the week fresh."
- "List quick cleaning tasks I can do in under 10 minutes."
- "Turn chores into a points-based game for my kids."

💰 Money, Budgeting & Planning

- "Create a simple household budget for $4,000 monthly income."
- "Help me plan for holiday spending on a $500 budget."
- "Suggest a savings strategy for irregular freelance income."

- "Explain interest and debt to a teenager in plain English."
- "Make a financial goals worksheet for me and my partner."

👨‍👩‍👧‍👦 Family & Personal Logistics

- "Plan a weekend getaway for a family of 5 on a budget."
- "Suggest family night ideas that don't involve screens."
- "Help me write a message for a babysitter explaining our bedtime routine."
- "Turn this chaotic week of appointments and errands into a clean calendar layout."
- "Create a checklist for getting kids ready for school in the morning."

🧠 Bonus Life Management Prompts

- "Act like a life coach. Help me simplify my weekly schedule."

- "You're a personal assistant—what should I prep for the week ahead?"

- "Help me build better routines with more rest and less stress."

- "Act like a professional organizer. Where do I even start with decluttering my house?"

✅ **Pro Tip**: Ask ChatGPT to format your routine or plan as:

- A checklist ✅

- A time-blocked schedule 🕐

- A printable list 🖨

- A shared doc 📑

- Or even a fun family challenge/game 🎯

Coming up next, we're zooming in on **parenting with AI**—how ChatGPT can be your co-pilot when you're juggling school runs, screen time battles, and helping with "new math." Whether you're a parent, guardian, or super involved aunt/uncle, you'll love what's in **Chapter 7**.

Chapter 7:

Parenting with AI — Because You Deserve Backup

If you're a parent, you already know: it's the most rewarding, exhausting, messy, incredible, emotionally complex job on Earth—and there's no manual.

Except now... maybe there kind of is?

Okay, not a full-on manual. But **ChatGPT can be a seriously useful tool in your parenting toolbox**—especially when it comes to juggling school stuff, answering "why" questions, keeping kids entertained, and sneaking in learning when screen time is inevitable.

This chapter is about **using AI to support you**, not replace you. Because parenting is still your gig—but it's totally okay to ask for help. Even if that help is an AI that can write bedtime stories and explain algebra at 9 PM when your brain has fully powered down.

📚 1. Homework Help (That Doesn't Make You Google Everything)

Kids ask great questions. Also: very confusing ones.

ChatGPT can help break things down in a way that actually makes sense to *them* (and to you).

Prompts to try:

- "Explain long division to a 10-year-old using pizza slices."
- "Help my 6th grader write a 5-paragraph essay about photosynthesis."
- "Create a multiple-choice quiz to study the planets."
- "Rewrite this science paragraph using simpler language."
- "Turn this historical topic into a fun story: [e.g., the Boston Tea Party]."

Need help checking work or proofreading? You can say:

"Check this paragraph for grammar and help make it clearer."

Suddenly, you're not just helping with homework—you're a homework hero.

2. Bedtime Stories, Made Just for Them

You know what never gets old? Personalized bedtime stories. And now you don't have to come up with them while half-asleep.

Try:

- "Write a short bedtime story about a shy dinosaur who learns to dance."
- "Tell a story where my son Max and our dog Luna go on a space adventure."
- "Create a silly rhyming story about a giraffe who opens a pizza restaurant."

You can make them magical, educational, funny, calming—whatever fits the vibe.

Bonus: Ask ChatGPT to turn the story into a little script and act it out with your kid. Big win.

🧠 3. Learning, Games & Screen Time That Doesn't Rot Their Brain

Need to keep them busy *and* learning? ChatGPT's your secret weapon.

Prompts:

- "Create a fun word game for a 7-year-old who loves animals."
- "Suggest five quiet indoor activities for a rainy day."
- "Write a riddle game that teaches basic math."
- "List 10 screen-free activities for an energetic 5-year-old."
- "Give me ideas for an educational YouTube-style quiz show we can do at home."

It can even generate scavenger hunts, trivia questions, and craft instructions. It's like Pinterest, minus the overwhelming perfection.

💬 4. Talking About Big Feelings (Or Tough Topics)

Sometimes kids ask questions that go *deep*. ChatGPT can help you start those conversations with more confidence.

Try:

- "How can I explain divorce to a 6-year-old in a gentle, reassuring way?"
- "Help me talk to my teenager about social media safety."
- "Write a short explanation of anxiety for a 10-year-old."
- "Create a list of affirmations for kids struggling with confidence."

And if *you* need help processing something first? Ask it to help you think it through before you even talk to your child.

5. Organizing Your Parent Life

Between permission slips, birthday parties, appointments, and "what day is it again?" chaos, ChatGPT can help you stay sane.

Prompts:

- "Make a checklist for back-to-school prep with two kids."
- "Help me plan a stress-free birthday party for a 5-year-old."

- "Turn my weekly family schedule into a printable calendar."
- "Suggest a system for organizing school papers, art, and permission slips."

You can even build a "Sunday family reset" routine together and stick to it (well, mostly).

🧠 Real Talk: AI Isn't Replacing You (and Shouldn't Try To)

ChatGPT is awesome at generating ideas, explanations, and tools—but it's not a replacement for *you*. The emotional connection, the hugs, the silly voices, the wisdom, the comfort? That's the human part. And it's irreplaceable.

Let ChatGPT take care of some of the *thinking* so you can focus more on the *loving*.

✅ Try This Before the Next Chapter:

1. Ask ChatGPT to write a short story for your kid—use their name, favorite animal, or toy.
2. Help with one school-related task (homework explanation, essay, quiz prep).

3. Try one fun activity idea, game, or weekend plan from its suggestions.

See what sticks—and keep building your own parenting "prompt vault."

Parenting Prompts Cheat Sheet

Use ChatGPT to support learning, spark creativity, and stay organized—without losing your mind.

📚 Homework Help & Learning

- "Explain long division to a 10-year-old using pizza slices."

- "Help my 3rd grader write a paragraph about the water cycle."

- "Create a quiz about the planets with 5 multiple-choice questions."

- "Turn this science explanation into kid-friendly language: [paste text]."

- "Make a short story that teaches the concept of recycling."

🌙 Bedtime Stories & Creative Fun

- "Write a bedtime story about a dog who becomes friends with a dragon."

- "Create a personalized adventure story starring [child's name] and their favorite toy."

- "Make a silly rhyming story that ends with a lesson about kindness."

- "Write a calming story for a child who's nervous about school."

- "Tell a short tale about a superhero whose power is cleaning up messes."

🧠 Games, Activities & Screen-Free Fun

- "List 10 rainy day activities for a 5-year-old with lots of energy."

- "Create a scavenger hunt using common things around the house."

- "Make a word game for an 8-year-old who loves animals."

- "Give me 5 ideas for educational games using just paper and crayons."

- "Suggest screen-free evening routines for a family with two kids."

💬 Tough Conversations & Big Feelings

- "How do I explain anxiety to a 9-year-old in a gentle way?"
- "Write a short explanation of what empathy means for a young child."
- "Help me talk to my child about divorce with reassurance and age-appropriate language."
- "Create affirmations for kids who are feeling overwhelmed."
- "How can I explain bullying to my child in a way they'll understand?"

📅 Family Life Organization

- "Create a checklist for back-to-school prep for two elementary-aged kids."
- "Plan a low-stress birthday party for a 6-year-old with a space theme."
- "Build a weekly family routine with work, homework, dinner, and playtime."
- "Make a printable visual chore chart for kids aged 6 and 10."

- "Help me organize school papers, art, and permission slips into a simple system."

Bonus Role-Based Prompts

- "Act like a child psychologist—how should I respond when my child says they feel left out at school?"

- "Pretend you're a kindergarten teacher—give me fun learning games using everyday objects."

- "You're a camp counselor—what are 5 ways to keep kids entertained on a long car trip?"

- "Act like a bedtime storyteller. Give me 3 magical stories for kids afraid of the dark."

Pro Tips for Parents:

- Always personalize prompts with your child's name, age, interests, or routines for extra magic.

- Turn ChatGPT's stories and games into real-life activities (print them, act them out, draw them).

- Keep a running doc or notebook called **"Family Prompt Vault"** for quick wins when you're busy or burned out.

Chapter 8:

ChatGPT – Your Personal Growth & Hobby Buddy

Let's talk about you for a minute.

Not your inbox. Not your job. Not your to-do list. Just... *you*.

Whether you want to journal more, build better habits, learn something new, or make time for a creative hobby— you don't have to do it all on your own. ChatGPT can actually be a really solid sidekick for your personal goals and passions.

Let's look at how to turn this AI tool into your own mini life coach, creativity spark, and learning buddy.

🧠 1. Build Better Habits

Struggling to stick with new routines? ChatGPT can help you:

- Break down a big goal into small daily habits
- Schedule those habits into your actual life
- Check in and hold yourself accountable

Try prompts like:

- "Help me build a morning routine that includes journaling, stretching, and 10 minutes of reading."
- "My goal is to drink more water and walk daily. Can you suggest a weekly tracker I can follow?"
- "Act like a productivity coach and help me stop procrastinating on my personal projects."

✍️ 2. Journal with a Buddy

Journaling is easier (and more fun) when someone prompts you with interesting questions. ChatGPT can:

- Ask thoughtful daily or weekly reflection questions
- Help you process thoughts, emotions, and decisions

- Summarize your journal entries to highlight growth over time

Prompts to try:

- "Ask me 3 questions to help me reflect on this past week."
- "Help me write a letter to my future self 6 months from now."
- "Guide me through a gratitude journaling session."

3. Learn Something New

Want to explore a topic or skill but don't know where to begin? ChatGPT can be your tutor, explainer, and quizmaster.

Ask it to:

- Break down complex topics into beginner-friendly steps
- Recommend resources or learning paths
- Create practice quizzes to help you study

Prompts to try:

- "Teach me the basics of photography, one step at a time."

- "Quiz me on Spanish vocabulary words for travel."

- "I want to learn about mindfulness. Can you give me a simple weekly plan?"

4. Get Creative with Hobbies

Whether you love writing, drawing, crafting, or something totally offbeat, ChatGPT can:

- Brainstorm ideas and project prompts
- Co-write stories or poems
- Help outline creative goals

Try these prompts:

- "Give me a daily drawing challenge for the next 7 days."

- "I want to write a short story. Help me come up with a plot and characters."

- "Act like a songwriting partner and help me brainstorm lyrics for a chill acoustic song."

5. Boost Wellness & Mindset

Need to reduce stress, improve sleep, or take better care of yourself? ChatGPT can:

- Build simple wellness routines
- Provide daily affirmations
- Guide you through mindfulness exercises

Prompt ideas:

- "Create a 10-minute evening routine that helps me wind down."
- "Give me 3 positive affirmations to start my day."
- "Help me journal through a tough day with encouraging questions."

🛠 Quick Wins: Build a Personal Growth Toolkit

Want to make this part of your regular routine? Try:

- Saving your favorite prompts to reuse each week
- Creating a custom journal structure with ChatGPT

- Checking in with your goals monthly and asking ChatGPT for progress feedback

Power Starter Prompts:

- "Check in with me each Sunday night and help me plan a balanced week."
- "Help me reflect on how I'm doing with my goals this month."
- "I need a little motivation today—can you give me a pep talk?"

Personal growth doesn't have to be a solo project. ChatGPT won't replace your inner work, but it can give you structure, inspiration, and support exactly when you need it.

Use it to make your life a little brighter, one prompt at a time.

Chapter 9:

Real Connections, Real Conversations – Using ChatGPT to Support Your Relationships & Social Life

Let's face it—relationships can be messy. Whether it's texting a new crush, sending a thank-you note to a friend, or navigating a tough talk with your partner, it's easy to get stuck wondering, *"How do I say this?"*

Good news: you don't have to figure it all out alone.

While ChatGPT isn't a substitute for actual human connection (and definitely not a licensed therapist), it *can* help you communicate more clearly, confidently, and kindly. Think of it as your personal messaging coach—ready to help you write the right words, anytime.

Whether you're deepening your closest relationships or just trying not to sound awkward on a dating app, this chapter will show you how ChatGPT can help you show up more thoughtfully in your social life.

💬 1. Say What You Mean (Without Overthinking It)

Ever reread a text or email 14 times before hitting send? Yeah... same.

Let ChatGPT help take the pressure off.

Try:

- "Help me write a kind message to a friend I haven't talked to in a while."
- "How do I say no to an invitation without sounding rude?"
- "Write a birthday message that's heartfelt but not too cheesy."
- "I need to apologize to my partner for being short-tempered. Can you help me write it?"

You can tweak tone, length, even add humor or emojis.

"Make this more casual."
"Add a bit of humor."
"Sound more sincere and warm."

Suddenly, sending thoughtful messages doesn't feel so stressful.

🩶 2. Handle Tricky Conversations With More Confidence

From misunderstandings to big life talks, relationships require good communication—and that can be hard when emotions are high or words are hard to find.

ChatGPT can help you:

- Draft a message to smooth things over after a disagreement

- Explain how you're feeling in a clear, respectful way

- Set a boundary with kindness

- Prepare what to say in a face-to-face convo you're nervous about

Try prompts like:

- "I need to talk to my friend about how I felt left out recently. Can you help me write something that's honest but not accusatory?"

- "Help me write a text to my sibling asking for more space without starting an argument."

- "What's a gentle way to tell someone I'm not ready to date right now?"

You can also ask for a **conversation script** to practice how you'd say it out loud—so when the moment comes, you feel ready.

🙏 3. Boost the Good Stuff—Appreciation, Connection, and Small Gestures

Communication isn't just about solving problems—it's also about *building closeness*. ChatGPT is great at helping you express appreciation, gratitude, or affection in ways that feel genuine.

Prompts to try:

- "Write a thank-you message to my neighbor for helping with yard work."

- "Help me write a sweet note to leave for my partner on a tough day."

- "What's a thoughtful message I can send to a friend going through a breakup?"

- "Give me a compliment that sounds personal and sincere, not generic."

Sometimes it's the small stuff—like remembering a birthday or following up after coffee—that makes the biggest impact. Let ChatGPT help you *show up* more often for the people you care about.

🩶 4. Dating? Flirting? Let AI Take the Edge Off

Yep, ChatGPT can help in your dating life, too. From writing bios to breaking the ice, it's a great wingman (minus the cheesy pick-up lines... unless you want those, too).

Examples:

- "Write a Tinder bio for someone who's into dogs, hiking, and rom-coms."

- "Suggest funny but respectful icebreakers for a dating app convo."

- "Help me reply to this message: 'Hey, you seem cool. What's your ideal weekend?'"

- "How do I politely let someone know I'm not feeling a spark?"

You can also ask it to rewrite your responses in a more engaging way, or check if a message sounds too formal (or too flirty). It's like having a chill friend on standby to sanity-check your love life.

🎉 5. Plan Hangouts, Events & Celebrations

Need help planning something fun? ChatGPT's great at brainstorming ideas for birthdays, group outings, date nights, and family get-togethers.

Prompts:

- "Plan a cozy at-home date night for two introverts on a budget."

- "Give me 5 group activity ideas for a friend reunion weekend."

- "Help me plan a fun surprise party for my partner's birthday."

- "What's a low-key way to celebrate my best friend getting a new job?"

It can even help write invites, create checklists, or suggest conversation starters if you're hosting a dinner or event.

🤝 6. Improve Your Communication Skills Over Time

Want to get better at expressing yourself in general? Use ChatGPT as a **practice partner**. Try:

- "Let's roleplay a tough conversation with a coworker."

- "Give me feedback on this message—does it sound passive-aggressive?"

- "Help me rewrite this email to be more clear and assertive."

- "Teach me how to use 'I' statements when I'm upset about something."

Over time, you'll build more confidence in your voice—and have a lot fewer moments where you think, *"Ugh, I should've said that differently."*

✅ Try This Before the Next Chapter:

1. Pick one relationship in your life—friend, partner, family member, coworker.

2. Ask ChatGPT to help you send them a kind, thoughtful message today (even just a check-in).

3. Or, if there's a convo you've been avoiding, try writing a practice message with ChatGPT's help—just to see how it feels.

Chapter 10:

Getting the Most from ChatGPT – Prompt Like a Pro,

Customize Like a Boss

By now, you've seen just how helpful ChatGPT can be—from planning your week and writing emails to telling bedtime stories and solving "what's for dinner" dilemmas.

But here's the secret: **you've only scratched the surface.**

In this final chapter, we're going to unlock a few advanced (but easy) techniques to help you level up your ChatGPT experience. Think of it as giving your AI assistant a bit of training—so it can understand *you*, your goals, your style, and your needs even better.

Whether you want to speed things up, add more personality, or create custom tools for work or life, this is where it all comes together.

💬 1. Prompting Like a Pro

Good prompts = great results. It's that simple.

Here's a quick cheat sheet to upgrade any prompt:

🧱 Structure it like this:

"You are [role]. Help me [task], with [specific details or goals]."

Examples:

- "You are a career coach. Help me update my resume for a marketing job with less than 5 years of experience."

- "Act like a nutritionist. Help me plan meals for a vegetarian trying to gain muscle."

- "You're a witty copywriter. Rewrite this product description with humor and energy."

The clearer your prompt, the better the output. Don't be afraid to:

- Add bullet points

- Give examples of what you like/don't like

- Use follow-ups: "Can you make that shorter/more casual/less formal?"

Remember: ChatGPT *wants* your feedback. Every prompt is a conversation, not a one-shot deal.

🧠 2. Use Memory (GPT-4 Users)

If you're using GPT-4, you can now **teach ChatGPT about you** using the built-in memory feature. This means it can remember:

- Your name
- Your writing style
- Your job, goals, or recurring projects
- Your preferences for tone, formatting, or types of advice

You can say:

"Hey, remember that I run a handmade candle business and I prefer friendly, upbeat copy."

Now, next time you say "Help me write a product description," ChatGPT will already know your context.

Memory saves time, makes the experience feel more personal, and helps ChatGPT grow with you.

Tip: Go to Settings > Personalization > Memory to turn it on or manage what it remembers.

💼 3. Build Your Own Mini-Tools with "Custom GPTs"

If you're using GPT-4, you also have access to **Custom GPTs**—your own personalized versions of ChatGPT that follow specific instructions, have unique behaviors, or include uploaded files and tools.

Think:

- A "RecipeBot" that only gives recipes based on your dietary preferences
- A "Resume Coach" GPT that formats everything the way you like
- A "Daily Planner" that opens every morning with your to-do template

You don't need to code—just click "Explore GPTs" inside ChatGPT, then "Create" your own. You'll fill in a few settings (like what it should sound like, or what it should always remember), and you're good to go.

If you find yourself doing the *same type of prompt* often, this feature will save you tons of time.

🔁 4. Create Prompt Templates You Can Reuse

Another easy "pro" trick? Save your best prompts as templates.

For example:

- **Daily reflection**: "Ask me 3 questions about my day. One about emotions, one about habits, one about gratitude."

- **Content idea generator**: "You're a social media strategist. Give me 5 content ideas about [topic]."

- **Meal planning**: "You're a nutrition coach. Plan 5 dinners this week for someone who eats gluten-free and wants 30-minute meals."

Keep your go-to prompts in a doc, Notes app, or even inside ChatGPT itself. Reusing them makes your workflow smooth and fast.

🔗 5. Integrate with Other Tools (If You're Feeling Fancy)

If you're tech-curious, ChatGPT can also work with tools like:

- **Zapier** or **Make.com** to automate tasks (e.g. turn ChatGPT responses into Google Docs, calendar entries, or Trello cards)

- **Google Sheets + GPT add-ons** to use ChatGPT inside a spreadsheet
- **Notion AI** if you're a Notion user—you can bring ChatGPT's power into your workspaces

This is optional! But it's there if you want to create a "second brain" that connects ChatGPT with your other digital tools.

🧠 6. Learn From Your Own Patterns

ChatGPT isn't just a tool—it's a *mirror*.

Over time, the way you use it will teach you:

- What matters to you
- What you avoid
- How you problem-solve
- What kinds of questions bring clarity

You might find that journaling with ChatGPT helps you process stress. Or that using it to prep for conversations makes you more confident. Or that letting it handle small decisions (like meal ideas or social captions) frees up brainpower for what really matters.

If you *let* ChatGPT be your sidekick—not your boss, not your crutch, but a steady, smart support system—you'll find your days just run a little smoother.

✅ Try This Before You Finish the Book:

1. Go back to your favorite chapters and copy 2–3 prompts you loved. Save them.

2. Create a "starter prompt" you can use each day or week (like journaling, planning, or content creation).

3. If you're using GPT-4, try turning on memory—or explore the GPT builder.

▦ Final Thoughts: You + ChatGPT = A Powerful Combo

This book wasn't about turning you into a robot—or turning ChatGPT into magic. It was about showing you what's possible when you bring *your human creativity, experience, and goals* together with a tool that helps you move faster, think clearer, and feel more supported.

ChatGPT isn't perfect. You'll still need to review, refine, and use your judgment. But if you use it well, it's like having an extra set of hands (and a surprisingly decent brain) on your team.

So now the only question is:
What will you use it for next?

Wrap-Up: You've Got the Tool —Now Make It Yours

You made it!
You've explored how ChatGPT can help you write, plan, learn, parent, grow, and breathe a little easier—both at work and at home.

The truth is, you don't need to *master* every feature to get massive value from this tool. You just need to start using it with *intention*.

Start small.
Start with what matters most to you right now.
Start with one prompt. One question. One moment of clarity.

ChatGPT is like a bike with no training wheels—it's ready to go whenever you are. You decide the pace. You decide the path. You decide the destination.

The more you use it, the more natural it will feel—and before you know it, you'll be doing things smarter, faster, and with way less mental clutter.

Remember: this isn't about doing more.
It's about making more room for what matters.

Let ChatGPT help you clear the noise, simplify the chaos, and create more space in your day, in your brain, and in your life.

Now... go make some magic.

⚡ The Power Prompts Toolkit

A few favorite prompts to copy, paste, and customize any time you need a boost.

🔄 Productivity & Planning

- "Help me prioritize this list of tasks and turn it into a realistic daily schedule: [paste list]."
- "What's one thing I can do today to make tomorrow easier?"
- "Act like a productivity coach. I have 3 big goals—how should I plan my week?"

🧠 Journaling & Mindset

- "Ask me 3 questions to help me reflect on my day."
- "What's something I did well today that I might be overlooking?"
- "Help me write a letter to my future self 3 months from now."
-

💡 Creativity & Hobbies

- "Give me a fun writing prompt that combines mystery and comedy."

- "Suggest a weekend DIY project using cardboard, string, and markers."

- "Create a 5-day photography challenge with a different theme each day."

💬 Social & Relationships

- "Help me write a kind message to reconnect with an old friend."

- "I need to set a boundary with someone—can you help me say it clearly but respectfully?"

- "What's a nice way to show appreciation to a partner who's had a rough week?"

🛒 Home & Life

- "Plan 5 dinners this week using ingredients I already have: [list ingredients]."

- "Create a family cleaning schedule that feels fair and doable."

- "Help me organize my weekend to include rest, errands, and a little fun."

🚀 Power Start Prompts

Use these to kick off your day or week:

- "What's one thing I should focus on this week, based on my goals?"

- "Give me a motivational message for today based on these priorities: [list them]."

- "Plan a calm, focused morning routine for me based on my schedule: [describe]."

💡 **Save these. Reuse them. Tweak them. Make them yours.**
ChatGPT is the tool—*you* are the magic behind it.

© **2025** ChatGPT Is My Co-Pilot: All rights reserved. No part of this publication may be reproduced, stored in a retrieval system, or transmitted in any form or by any means—electronic, mechanical, photocopying, recording, or otherwise —without the prior written permission of the author.

Printed in Dunstable, United Kingdom